How To Use Salamstore Quran Reading Pen!

By Salamstore

https://www.facebook.com/pg/erc1234567

https://www.amazon.com/dp/B07MRJCWKW

https://www.amazon.com/dp/B078VNDNPQ?

https://www.ebay.com/itm/Quran-Read-Pen/163596182524?hash=item261717a3fc:g:05IAAOSwzMlce3Hb

TABLE OF CONTENT

1.0 INTRODUCTION 3

1.1 INTRODUCTION TO AL-QUR'AN 4

   There were two distinct revelations of the Holy Qur'an 10

1.2 VIRTUES OF LEARNING HOW TO RECITE THE QUR'AN 13

   Virtues of learning how to recite the Qur'an 19

   TIPS ON HOW TO LEARN QUR'ANIC RECITATION 22

1.3 VIRTUES OF LISTENING TO THE QUR'AN 24

2.0 INTRODUCTION TO SALAMSTORE QURAN READING PEN 33

2.1 INTRODUCTION TO SALAMSTORE QUR'AN SPEAKER 38

2.2 HOW TO USE SALAMSTORE READING PEN TO LEARN HOW TO RECITE QUR' AN 42

2.3 HOW TO USE THE SALAM STORE SPEAKER TO LEARN HOW TO RECITE THE QUR'AN 46

3.0 LESSONS THAT CAN BE DERIVED FROM THE QUR'AN 47

1.0 INTRODUCTION

All praise and adorations belong to Almighty Allah the most beneficent, the most merciful that gave me the privilege to write this book on how to learn and recite the Holy Qur'an with Salam store pen and speaker.

The chapters of the book include a vivid explanation on the virtues of learning how to recite the Qur'an, and it also consists of the attributes bestowed on a Muslim that listens to the recitation of the Qur'an. Moreover, there is a chapter that gives insight about the two devices mentioned about, which are Salam store reading and Salam store speaker respectively.

The subsequent chapter explains how to use this device to learn how to recite the Qur'an and also how to listen to the Qur'an with the speaker.

I beseech Almighty Allah to bestow the blessing of whoever recite and listen to the Qur'an on us. Amin

1.1 INTRODUCTION TO AL-QUR'AN

Al-Qur'an is the seal of all divine book sent from Allah (SWT) for the emancipation of humankind through the archangel to our beloved prophet Muhammad(PBUH). We all know that there are several books sent from Allah (SWT) before the Qur'an, but Qur'an been the last contains all the contents of all the divine books sent before it and more. The Qur'an was sent as a blessing to the generality of the human

Al-Qur'an comprises of 114 chapters, and each chapter is included of individual verses. Chapter 2 which is the longest chapter of the glorious Qur'an has 286 verses and chapters

103, 108 and 110 are the shortest chapters with three verses each. The whole Qur'an contains 6,236 chapters in total.

86 of the 114 chapters were revealed in the first 12 years of prophethood when the prophet was in Mecca, and the other 28 chapters were revealed after the Prophet's migration to Madina. Most of the Madinite chapters contain much information because of the emerging Muslim community and the need to deal with different inter-personal relation issues. Also, the Madinite chapters occupy 40% of the Qur'an even though their number of chapters is less than the ones in Mecca.

The majority of the scholars agreed that the first verse revealed to the prophet (PBUH) was the first five verses of chapter 96 in cave Hira. The prophet (PBUH) was reported to visit the cave frequently before the Arch Angel Jibril visited him on that auspicious day with the revelation and the verses go thus in 96:1-5:

"Read [O Muhammad!] in the name of your Lord who created. He created man from a clot. Read, and your Lord is the Most Honorable. Who taught with the pen? Taught man what he knew not."

Moreover, the last verse that was revealed was chapter 2:281 as agreed by the majority of the scholars.

It is remarkable to know that chapter 1 of the complete Qur'an was not the first verse that was revealed and that chapter 114 was not the last chapter that was revealed. Also, to say a little thing about how the Qur'an was compiled to the form that we have today. We all know that the prophet

(PBUH) cannot read and write, but with the mercy of Almighty Allah, he has excellent scribers available around him.

When the revelation came to him, he read it out to his companions and ask Zaid bn Thabit to write in down on any material they find around such as bone, leaf, hides of animals and parchments, under his supervision. These scribes were kept in one corner in the prophet's room. While some of the companions memorized it with heart, the compilation of the Holy Qur'an was inspired by caliph Umar (may Allah be pleased with him) during his era as the leader of the Muslim community. He noticed that most of those that memorized the Qur'an are being killed during a battle with the non-believer. So, he called for the compilation on one slate.

Al-Qur'an relates the history of good and evil people and how Allah (SWT) rewarded the former and punished the latter so that our generation can learn from them. Al- Qur'an was revealed to the prophet (PBUH) who was an Arab, and the Arab is known for their eloquence and their exceptional skill in poetry.

Some of the leaders of the Quraish tribe, where the prophet (PBUH) hails from related the verses to be from a poet or a sorcerer. However, when it was related to some of their best poets, they were overwhelmed and said this is beyond the words of a man. Moreover, Allah (SWT) revealed a verse to support that in Quran 10:37-38

Almighty Allah promised to preserve the Qur'an against any alteration whatsoever, that why we have a unified Qur'an in every part of the world. The rhythmic pattern of the glorious

Qur'an makes it easy to memorize, which is the primary source of its preservation.

The Qur'an was revealed in the language of the last prophet. "Verily, we have sent it down as an Arabic Qur'an so that you may understand." (Qur'an 12: 2). The Qur'an is a permanent literary miracle that cannot be imitated. In spite of the literary power of the Quraysh, they were unable to produce a single verse like that of the Qur'an. This proves the miraculous nature of the Qur'an. Allah (S.W.T) said;

There were two distinct revelations of the Holy Qur'an

1. The descent of the Qur'an from (al-lawh al-mahfoodh) on which it was written, to the lowest Heaven, referred to as (Bayt al-izzah). Allah caused the Qur'an to descend on Laylatul-Qadr(the night of Decree), one of the odd-numbered

nights in the last ten days of the month of Ramadan. This is referred to as the first revelation.

2. The second revelation was being sent down by Allah through Archangel Jibril, to the prophet for 23 years.

The Qur'an was revealed to the prophet in seven different Arabian dialects (Quraysh, Hudhayl, Thaqeef, Hawazan, Kinanah, Tameem, and Yemen). Some Arabs began to boast that their dialect was superior over others.

When new Muslims made mistakes in their recitation of the Qur'an, it was sometimes difficult to tell whether it was incorrect or whether it was one of the seven reading thought by the Prophet.

The Qur'an as it is today was done during the caliph Uthman era. The compilation was done by Zaid ibn Thabit heading a committee of four Quranic Scholars.

All praises to Almighty Allah for his blessing on us and for the gift of Al-Qur'an, which is a source of healing for all humanity. It shouldn't surprise you that the Qur'an that was revealed to the prophet(PBUH) for over 1400 years ago is still the same Qur'an we have with us today free from faults and any alteration as Allah said Qur'an chapter 15:9 that " Verily, it is We who revealed the Remembrance [the Qur'an], and verily, We are its Guardian."

This guidance is only synonymous to the Qur'an alone and not to other Arabic text or the Ahadith of the prophet (PBUH).

1.2 VIRTUES OF LEARNING HOW TO RECITE THE QUR'AN

Muslim all over the world learns how to recite the Qur'an in order to complete their obligations as a believer. Though, some find it hard to learn how to recite due to, lack of tutors or lack of spare time to reach a learned person to teach them. I believe after going through this piece, which will highlight the virtues of learning how to recite the Qur'an and living by its understanding. This will awaken the spirit of learning how to recite this glorious book. However, a device is going to be introduced in subsequent chapters in the book that can ease the hitch of learning how to recite Al-Qur'an.

When you listen to the Qur'an, all you hear is the cure to our depression-stricken world, what about when you read? You see the answer to all our questions beautifully written word after word; words that transcend your understanding most majestically.

The Qur'an was revealed over 1400 years ago, a divine revelation to the seal of the prophets, from the highest and mighty. Allah sent down the book as guidance and mercy to all humanity. Allah says "Here is a plain statement to men, a guidance and instruction to those who fear Allah" and no one turns away from this book except that he leads a depressing life.

To read the Qur'an is to open doors to guidance and listen to it while it's being recited is to let open the vault of tranquility. There are a million and one virtues that come along with reading the Qur'an. These are plain words that we come across when we recite the Qur'an.

It is a blessing upon us and that by way of this we are admonished. Admonitions on how we are to lead our lives up until the day of recompense. Admonition on what truly matters in life and how to stay focused in order not to be swerved away by the waves of distractions that rack our existence. How beautifully organized and well lived would our lives be, if we are to turn to the Qur'an not just reading but to live by its understanding and implementation.

Many walks around with hearts filled with pits and with no idea on how to ease themselves of the worries that haunt them. It all lies in the Qur'an the words of reassurance and hope that Allah accepts your repentance no matter what sin you commit and no matter how deep you are in it and such are the words that we find in the Quran when we pay attention to it.

Another benefit of reading the Qur'an is that it's just an excellent way to amass rewards to know that each letter that is recited has ten rewards attached to it. I mean what unique way to get lots if rewards than this. Yes, whosoever reads a letter from the book of Allah, he will have a, and that reward will be multiplied by 10. And no matter how difficult it is to try, the best part is that even while you find it difficult to recite, you have a double reward. Glory be to Allah as our creator wants nothing but good for us.

Apart from reciting the Qur'an yourself, listening to the Qur'an brings such tranquility that you can never find anywhere else. May Allah make it easy for us to be from the companion of the Qur'an and to be from those who will discover the pleasure of Allah through it because none shall hold on to the book of Allah except that he finds the joy of the Almighty.

Al-Qur'an is a divine revelation from our creator to solve all human-related problems. Allah (SWT) said in the Glorious Qur'an that "This book (Al-Qur' an), of which there is no doubt, guidance to those who are pious." (Qur'an 2:2)

This is to show that reciting the Qur'an can lead to being conscious of Allah, which will make us entitled to the guidance as said by Almighty Allah in the verse above.

Also, Uthman (may Allah be pleased with him) narrates that the Prophet (PBUH) said: "The best amongst you is he who learns the Qur'an and teaches it." (Bukhari, Abu Dawud, Tirmidhi)

It is rewarding to know that learning how to recite the Qur'an and teaching it is a great act encouraged by the prophet (PBUH)

Virtues of learning how to recite the Qur'an

There are numerous virtues narrated from the Prophet (PBUH) and also from the Qur'an, which we are just going to look into very few of them. Reciting the Qur'an purifies the soul just as sponge and soap purify the body. A soul that does not listen or recite the Qur'an is like a dead soul, and a soul that recites or listen to the Qur'an is like a soul that is alive.

1. RECITING THE QUR' AN COMPLETES A MUSLIM OBLIGATION

As we all know that Islam is a religion of sincerity, sincerity to what? Sincerity to Allah, the Prophet, the book (Qur'an), the leader and the common. Then, how can we be sincere to the book? We can be sincere to the book reciting, listing and reflecting on the meaning of the Qur'an and also, making sure its teaching reflects in our actions. Moreover, teaching it is also one of the acts of being sincere to the Qur'an, and by doing this, a Muslim has fulfilled his obligation.

2. THE QUR' AN WILL ACT AS AN INTERCESSOR

On the day of accountability, where no wealth or post will be of use to the owner the Qur'an will come as an intercessor on behalf of all those that recite it on earth.

3. ELEVATED STATUS ON EARTH

The status of whosoever recites the Qur'an is elevated among human as Umar (may Allah be pleased with him) that the Prophet (PBUH) said: "Allah raise some people's status by this book and lowers others by it."

4. THERE IS REWARD FOR EVERY LETTER RECITED FROM THE QUR'AN

For every letter of the Qur'an been recited there is a reward for it by Almighty Allah, especially the one recited in Ramadan. Even there is more reward for those that struggle in the pronunciation of the words. The Prophet was reported to have said "Whosoever reads a letter from the Book of Allah (Al-Qur' an), he will have a reward. Moreover, that reward will be multiplied by ten."

5. THE QUR' AN WILL LEAD ITS RECITERS TO PARADISE

After acting as an intercessor for its reciter, the Qur'an will also lead its reciter to the paradise, when all other people are finding it hard to find their way through the thin line between hell and paradise. The Prophet said "The Qur'an is an intercessor, something has given permission to intercede, and it is rightfully believed in. Whosoever puts it in front of him, and it will lead him to Paradise; whosoever puts it behind him, it will steer him to the Hellfire."

With all these highlighted virtues I urge my Muslim brothers and sisters to hold the Qur'an tight and be steadfast in our pursuit in seeking for the knowledge of Quranic recitation.

TIPS ON HOW TO LEARN QUR'ANIC RECITATION

Many people began to memorize the whole Qur'an without understanding a word of what they had memorized.

The recitation of the Qur'an is used in worship(salah).

The Quran explains (tells us) about the incident of the past, the present and predicts the future.

There is no book, religious or otherwise, which has been memorized compared to the number that has memorized the Qur'an. The Qur'an is about four-fifths the length of the New Testament of the Christians, yet not a single person in recorded history is known to have memorized the New Testament completely.

The word Qur'an in its context means "reading" or "recitation." The first verse revealed was; "Read! In the name of your Lord, who has created (all that exists)" (Qur'an 96: 1).

The Prophet encourages us to read all of it (the Qur'an) once per month if we can.

Scholars who specialized in the recitation of the Qur'an recitation formulated rules of reading (the science of Tajwid) based on the authentic recitation which they had learned.

Recitation of the Qur'an is a means by which the message can be absorbed.

Umar ibn al-Khattab is reported to have said: "Learn the Qur'an five verses at a time, for verily, Jibril used to descend with the Qur'an for the Prophet five at a time." This method can also be abducted.

1.3 VIRTUES OF LISTENING TO THE QUR'AN

The Qur'an has revealed to the prophet Muhammad (PBUH) as a blessing and guidance to humanity. It was revealed in parts and not complete as it today. The intent of Allah (SWT) was for the messenger to read it to his followers. The listen to him and act upon what he interpreted to them of the Qur'an, and in return, it increases their faith and makes them a better Muslim.

It take a little bit of calmness to listen to the Qur'an unlike reciting it on your own, while listening to the Qur'an the ear, brain, and heart need to be alert in order to gain the benefits of the person who listens the Qur'an unlike reading where the eye, mind, ear, and heart are the primary organs needed.

The virtues of listening to the Qur'an should not be underestimated, because as bathing the body cleanses the body and prevents it from bacteria and what could deteriorate the skin. The same effect goes with the listening of the Qur'an as it replenishes the soul and keeps it in the right conditions.

Allah (SWT) commanded the Muslim only to read or listen to the Quran but also to understand its meaning. Because it contains healing, blessing and also will help us to know the tenets of our religion and its impact on our lives.

The verse above shows the effect of listening to the recitation of the Holy Qur'an, as it helps a believer to understand the sovereignty of Allah and also, how to worship him alone. However, it also shows us that Allah forgives our sins when we seek forgiveness.

Also, listening to the Qur'an improves our understanding that the words are from the creator of the heaven and the earth and not mere words of a human being. Because it has emotional benefits as it brings us closer to our creator.

Allah also said in Qur'an 7:204 that "When the Qur'an is read, listen to it with attention, and remain silent, that you may receive mercy." So, I will like to point out some of the virtues of listening to the Qur'an in details.

1. LISTENING TO THE QUR'AN CAN CURE DAMAGED BRAIN CELLS

The Qur'an as said earlier that, it is a blessing to humanity. One of its benefits is that it can cure damaged brain cells. Brain cells damaged by viruses and bacteria can be cured by listening to the Holy Qur'an. The sound of the Qur'an halts the viruses and bacteria activities and also increases the functionality of the healthy cells to fight against the viruses.

The sound of the Qur'anic verses creates a pitch that enters the ear and move to the brain to influence the brain cells through the electromagnetic field generated from the tone. The brain cells respond to the electromagnetic field to change the vibration of the cells to cure the damaged brain cells.

This is the natural phenomenon created by Almighty Allah in the brain cell. Allah said in Qur'an 30: 30 that "Then face your face straight to [Allah's] religion; the fithrah of God who created a man according to the fithrah. There is no change in the fithrah of God. That is the righteous religion, but most humans do not know. "

2. IT REDUCES STRESS

Listening to the Holy Qur'an create a sensation in the body as if it's in the state of rest. In this state, the cells send a signal to the sensory gland in the body to secrete hormones. This hormone keeps the body relaxed and stress-free as if the person is doing therapy.

3. SERVES AS CURE FROM SICKNESS

The virtues of listening to the Qur'an is proved by field of medicine as medical practitioners explained that the cells in the body vibrate in a specific pattern. Any change in this pattern will cause illness in that part of the body as a result of a damaged cell.

The damaged cells can be vibrated back to regain balance. To make this sound is continuously required. So, reciting the Qur'an makes a tremendous impact in the brain cells to restore balance. More researches show that cancer cells can be destroyed by using sound frequency, and again it was proved that the sound from the Quranic verses has an impact in healing diseases of cancer caliber. Viruses and bacteria stop activities while Qur'an is being recited and makes healthy brain cells function well.

4. INCREASES CREATIVITY

People who are conversant with listening to the recitation of AL Qur'an will have high retention memory. High retention memory makes it easy to memorize things, in turn, enhances intelligence and improves creativity.

5. IT HAD POSITIVE IMPACT ON THE HEALTH OF ORGANS

A researcher Dr. Ahmed Al-Qazi said in the outcome of his research that listening to the recitation of the Qur'anic verse, reduces tension of the muscles in the body and also the heart impulse becomes manual.

You may be surprised that the science backed the sayings of the Holy Qur'an, but I would love to tell you not to because it is the words of the Lord of the universe.

2.0 INTRODUCTION TO SALAMSTORE QURAN READING PEN

Salamstore Qur'an reading pen is a beautifully crafted pen-like designed device with fantastic functionality. The functionalities include:

1. it can read any verse of the Qur'an by touching it with each word on the page.

2. it contains voice recitation of the Holy Qur'an by great Imams.

3. it has audio translations with not more than 30 language options including English, Urdu, and French.

4. it can record/translate and repeat recitation for easy memorization.

Salamstore

https://www.facebook.com/pg/erc1234567

https://www.amazon.com/dp/B07MRJCWKW

https://www.amazon.com/dp/B078VNDNPQ?

https://www.ebay.com/itm/Quran-Read-Pen/163596182524?hash=item261717a3fc:g:05IAAOSwzMlce3Hb

5. it can teach a user how to pray, and also it can recite the dua in each section of salah, from the athahiyat to salatul ibrahimiyah and some qunoot.

6. it has tafsir of all the verses in the Holy Qur'an, with this user can have a deep understanding of the Qur'an and by doing so it will ease its implementation.

7. it is very portable, which makes it easy for children and adult to recite Qur'an anywhere from their sdcard and with the mushaf.

8. it has a one-year warranty, so you don't need to panic, while using it.

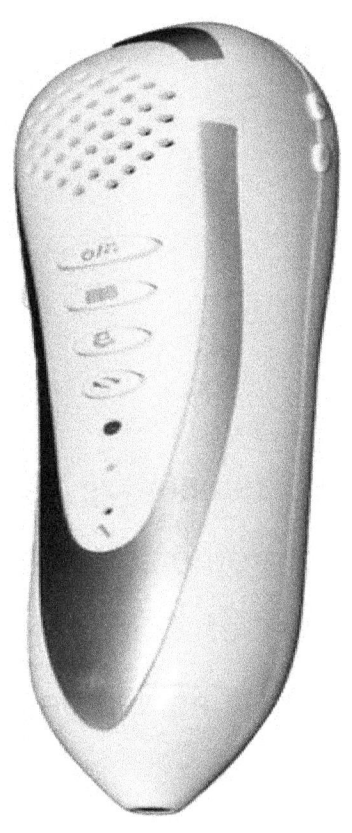

The smart designed pen-like designed device has an in-built speaker with a loud sound. It also comes with 8gb in-built flash memory; it also has a USB port for easy connection with a computer, it has an average of 6 hours working time when it is fully charged with its built Li battery.

2.1 INTRODUCTION TO SALAMSTORE QUR'AN SPEAKER

Salamstore Qur'an speaker is an attractive cylindrical shaped device with remote control, designed to ease learning and recitation of Qur'an for Muslim who want to complete their obligations as a believer.

Short Touch Change Brightness;
Touch 2 seconds to Switch to Color Light.

The speaker has many functionalities which include:

1. The speaker comes with 25 famous Qur'an reciters and 23 translation audios.

2. It also has Tafseer jalalain recitation for ease the understanding of a chapter or a verse before moving to the next chapter or verse.

3. The speaker also switches mode from single mode to double style. The double-mode includes recitation and translation or recitation and Tafseer.

4. the remote control makes it easy to control the device without having to move closer to it.

2.2 HOW TO USE SALAMSTORE READING PEN TO LEARN HOW TO RECITE QUR' AN

I will start by unwrapping the Salam store reading pen package to unveil the items in the box. The box includes Qur'an, the reading pen, an earpiece, a charger and a manual to make it easy to how to use the device efficiently. It also has a teacher manual to help understand how the verses and comprehension of the Qur'an are constructed. There's also a language guide and a reciter guide, whereby you choose a reciter from the manual and point it to the verses to listen to the reciter.

The Qur'an reading pen is a fantastic reading pen that is designed for anybody who wants to learn how to recite the Qur'an effectively. The powerful tools have a unique technology to scan and read any page, chapter, and verse in the Holy Qur'an. Just by pressing the pen on that portion of the page, the page number to listen to a page. Also, touch the name of the chapter to listen to the chapter. You can also listen to any page or any verse by touching the first letter of the page or verse. You can also press the repeat button on the pen to listen to the verse you just heard. Moreover, you can press the translation button to listen to the translation of the Ayah you just listened.

With the support provided by the Salam store reading pen saves people from embarrassment. Because, it gives a variety of translation languages like French, Urdu and other languages. Also, you can select from your favorite reciter to ease your learning process.

The pen improves reading and listening skills for all learners. You can also use the hands-free with the reading pen not to disturb people around you while learning with the reading pen.

The reading pen can improve readers' Qur'an reading skill vocabulary and enhances the understanding of Qur'an comprehension. Support your Qur'an reading with this breakthrough technology.

2.3 HOW TO USE THE SALAM STORE SPEAKER TO LEARN HOW TO RECITE THE QUR'AN

The speaker Qur'an has a screen that displays the Qur'an verse you are listening to. It has a forward and backward button. It also has a play/pause button. The mode button can allow you to choose from the Mp3 mode and radio mode. The forward button can be used to change the chapter the speaker will pronounce the name of the chapter selected, and the display screen displays the chapter number you are listening to.

You can change to Ayah number with the remote to know the verse you are listening to. You can use the handsfree to listen to it alone. The remote can also be used to change reciter to your favorite reciter. Also, you can use the remote to choose the translation with the speaker. You can also listen to the Arabic recitation and translation, which you can set with the remote.

3.0 LESSONS THAT CAN BE DERIVED FROM THE QUR'AN

As discussed earlier the Qur'an has numerous lesson that can be derived from it, because it is a book that was sent from Allah (SWT) for the deliverance of humanity.

The Qur'an is applicable today as it was three millennia before now, it is a companion that guides believer on their day to day affairs. The Qur'an should be taken as a friend, i.e., it should be read and reflected upon every day, so that the reader can feel the impact.

Here are some lessons that can be derived from the Qur'an.

I want you to know that all the lessons enumerated below are just a few compared to the pool of lessons that contained in the Qur'an.

1. GRATITUDE

The opening verse of the glorious Qur'an emphasized on giving appreciation and gratitude to the lord of the universe for all his blessings on us. Instead of complaining about our predicament, it provides us with the opportunity of looking at our lives in another perspective by thanking Allah for the gift of health, faculties of thinking, breath and being alive at this time. Most of these things are what we humans don't see as blessings, and indeed they are gifts from our Lord.

As Allah said in Qur'an 14:7 that "And [remember] when your Lord proclaimed, 'If you are grateful, I will surely increase you [in favor] ..."

This shows that by proclaiming appreciation to Almighty Allah for his blessings on us, he (Allah) will increase the benefit in many folds. However, in any predicament we find ourselves, we need to be grateful to Almighty Allah.

2. INTENTION

The prophet(PBUH) said in a hadith reported by Umar(may Allah be pleased with him) that "All actions are judged according to intention." and as we all that we were created for worshiping Allah alone as it was stated in Qur'an 51:56 "And I did not create the jinn and mankind except to worship Me." Having a purified intention makes the worship of a Muslim acceptable by Almighty Allah.

Also, purifying intention does not stop at worship only; it also extends to our daily life. When we decide to achieve a goal, it is essential to have a good intention and stick to the dream of attaining it.

3. KNOWLEDGE

The Holy Qur'an reinstated the need for knowledge in this era; that's why the first revelation was "Iqra" meaning read. Knowledge is what differentiate between truth and falsehood. However, it is also the antidote for ignorance, because an ignorant does more harm to himself and the community at large.

Seeking knowledge is incumbent on all Muslims including male and female. In the Qur'an, there are numerous du'a that shows how to supplicate to Almighty Allah for an increase in knowledge. As the prophet (PBUH) was commanded in the Quran to say "My Lord Increase me, and increase me in knowledge." Qur'an 20:114.

4. DEDICATION, AND PATIENCE

We learn from the story of the prophet (PBUH) how we were a dedication to his mission and how he persevered through a hard time. Also, how he was patient through the struggle, and how his efforts were crowned with success. The example shows us that Muslims can achieve their dream, when they are dedicated, hardworking and have the patience to persevere through the process. Allah (SWT) said in the Glorious Qur'an that "Spend the night awake in prayer, except for a little bit of sleep." (73:2)

Spending the part of the night to pray about our situations can go a long way in solving it. Depriving yourself of sleep is a sign of dedication as shown in verse.

The above lessons are not all that can be found in the Qur'an but it just to show a little of the morals and experiences that a Qur'an reciter can benefit from their recitation.

Salamstore

https://www.facebook.com/pg/erc1234567

https://www.amazon.com/dp/B07MRJCWKW

https://www.amazon.com/dp/B078VNDNPQ?

https://www.ebay.com/itm/Quran-Read-Pen/163596182524?hash=item261717a3fc:g:05IAAOSwzMlce3Hb

Andrei Besedin©

Ingram Content Group UK Ltd.
Milton Keynes UK
UKHW051918200323
418860UK00012B/447